BLINDSIDE

Deer Dan,   2020
Happy birthday,
my love,
                lov
Sydney (+Dublin + London ...

By the same author:

Poetry

Bitter Suite (1995)
Parochial (2000)
A Difficult Faith (2006)
Looking Out from Bashan: the republic of Og (2012)

BLINDSIDE

Mark Reid

PUNCHER & WATTMANN

First published in 2018
Published by Puncher and Wattmann
PO Box 441
Glebe NSW 2037

http://www.puncherandwattmann.com

puncherandwattmann@bigpond.com

National Library of Australia
Cataloguing-in-Publication entry:

Reid, Mark

Blindside

ISBN   9781925780017

I. Title.

A821.3

Cover design by David Musgrave

This project has been assisted by the Australian Government through the Australia Council, its arts funding and advisory body.

Contents

I

II

III

IV

I see men as trees, walking

Mark 8:24

I

What is the sound of one hand clapping?

I am appalled to find myself
this literal
but still don't really get it.

When first put to me
I just hold up my right hand
cupped, & rapidly
work the fingers, their tips
patting anxious, frenetic
against the Mount of Venus.

It makes a thin papery sound
but is clapping of a sort,
if not the rousing
ovation on its feet,
the auditorium itself
in crescendo.

No, it makes one lone
& scrambled fretting,
a stricken, spasmodic
binary code;

but then the sun suddenly hits me
& I look up at the room,
at that window flooding light,
an open-curtained stage

at which I wildly,
singly, applaud.

Eavesdropping

If a tree falls in the forest
the possum hears. A roo stands
alert & still, twitches then lopes
away.

The wombat curled
in his shuddering burrow
covers his ears, & galahs, as if
thrown into the sky, they
hear it too & everyone
hears galahs.

But sound is no democracy.

There are exclusive pitches
denied to us,
there is a nature beyond.

We listen, we strain,
hear only the panicking birds.

The War of Independence

quoting Tertullian

Donald Rumsfeld, U.S. Secretary
of Defense, made mention

of *known unknowns*,
as if military intelligence

were a theological proof.
My mother said once

of a certain friend she
thought the world of him.

I thought all the people
of all the world thought

the world of all the people.
I thought of those thoughtful worlds,

I thought of the accident we passed,
the man with blood on his head,

the little boy over the road
drowned in the neighbours' pool;

thoughtful worlds
lighting all those windows.

When we lived in town
the streetlights went out at ten.

Dad was walking home
pissed with a baguette

when the police-spot hit.
I am armed sir with bread-stick -

batter my heart!
I was thinking of thinking

something unthinkable,
I was thinking a known unknown;

like Darwin in his infancy,
Washington at his cherry tree,

that long sequence of chimpanzees,
each one of me standing taller.

Induction

This was being a man:
to go to the Barber, even
if it was your mother
who took you.

Four chairs, four Barbers, four
Barbers' chairs in a row on the lino,
four Barbers lined in a row,
white Barbers' coats like Doctors'.

Mum wouldn't allow a crew-cut,
no matter what some kids had. I had
the part & the wave & she'd stop,
fix it a little, right there in the street.

But there I was, being a man,
waiting with the others
on a bench against a wall,

sitting in a row
mirrored back to myself.

Housekeeping

A predator sleeps
as a mother sleeps,
listening still.

In the cornice
above my bed
she has set up house,

long-legged,
thin-waisted, poised
on her canny wires

as the hand
of the pianist
is poised.

Here
is the grace
of the innate,

hers is
singular
knowledge.

She conjures a ball,
white,
a small round cloud.

It is her pearl,
from the arachnid heart.
She clasps

this treasure to her
as the setting
clasps the jewel:

love proceeds
concentric
with this meditation.

This morning
a world
has come into being,

is breathlessly
carried,
with not a word,

with blind creative will,
this puff-ball
explosion of tiny spiders

shimmering in the web,
each one busy
devouring the others.

Future eating

Acts XI

And we no more than picnickers
looking for the ideal spot;
where best to throw a rug,
square on square of billowing tartan,
let down by four corners.

We think over there might be better,
or there, or perhaps by the creek would be nice -
o no - look - ants!

As if we could once be satisfied, say

yes, this is good, this will do

& lifting the lid of our basket wherein -
every beast, every fowl, every creeping thing.

The Devil & James Dickey

Shadow is the first
function of light, & the
silhouette of a plane,
the clean lines of a raptor,
signals dread. At least
to us creatures on the ground.

And for Dickey himself,
replicated in the cockpit,
knowing what to do,
be doing, have done.

We are so far beneath
him & his sincerity,
his duty, his resolve.

All his wordiness
rains down on us.
He does what he does.
Done.

Let him wake then
always to that likeness.

Let no one comfort him,
say ...*shhh...now...*

let verse be the simulator,
the man turning on himself,
counting his kills;

let that be the bullet he takes.

The startled tarmac clears.
Conscience winds its props.
The choice is between
choice & none,
the shadow of a wingspan
over rooftops, smoke, eruption.

Then turning, banking away,
wings tilting with such grace
you'd think the aesthetic
might redeem him.

Death song

The spot hits
& so does the shot -
between the eyes.

A roo stands
& drops, as if
by the hand of God.

It is a celebrated
conjunction of
dog meat, sport &

lookin' after the farm
executed off
an unroadworthy ute.

The dogs gnaw all night,
fur & all.

Fremantle elegy

Things return to much
as they were when she rang,
the dishes in the sink.

She said she hated to tell me,
to be the one, she said
she'd done her screaming.

Shock is a physical understanding,
the hand holding the receiver,
the shaft of the body
through which words fall,

fail, or are overwhelmed
by things inert, things
that I wake to find,
the bottles I
toasted you with.

This imperative of objects
is our one labour,
it is pain's information,
the body's pilot

& I, for one,
am returning to the things,
to the dishes, the poems,
the hangover. I will
perform the chores, take
the pleasures, wash, eat &
tidy up;

I will have my suit dry-cleaned
because you were done
with things & possibility,
the wilful body,
that saboteur,
thought.

But in the front room
of her semi-detached,
winter squalls
raining in off the shipyards,

she would hold me
in that tantrum night,
hold me
as she would hold you;

& I would fold
back into those sheets
& think of you
in the same rocked bed, think
of you thinking of me.

I would think of us as intimates.

The Burke & Wills Fan Club

Who noticed it first? How
a view will keep backing off,
meaning we might walk forever,
always push a little further, that
horizon lifting, dipping like hope,
& we, as if in a straight line,
we keep going, going
for the delusion, the mirage,
the twin palms, shade & pool.
In the *MONKEES* movie a
thirsting Mickey Dolenz finds
a *Coca-Cola* machine in the desert.
That's cool but the gag depends
entirely, for us, on the telling.
We believe anything well told.
We believe what Mickey believes.
We believe
in that *Coca-Cola* machine.
Last night I turned off the tv
& sat out on the verandah
looking off at the cliche stars.
Mickey, you guessed it,
has no change.

Freud's fraud

We must not, cannot
trust.

Beware the mind,
beware the dark persuasion.

The mind gives false direction.

The mind
has a secret automation.

The mind
will drive you over the edge.

So this the old bus of the breast,
this the Oedipal Lotus,
this our limousine of transference,
the torn mother huffing in the tuck shop;

whatever we think,
the mind is talking dirty.

We cannot, must not
trust & yet,
in our failed & heartfelt artworks

we offer up
the disembodied phenomena
into which we divide.

We sit thinking in traffic.

We sit thinking in traffic
as the traffic itself,

with its crimes of association,
thinks.

It gets no more real.

The meter is running.

The idiot at the wheel
remains hidden.

An etymology of terror

with a line from Solsbury Hill

Who knows what
is buried where?

Any step
may trip the wire.

Any step
may be the misstep.

However plain, however hidden,
any word
may be a weapon against me,
me the conscript,
without immunity.

Rusting perhaps
from a cold conflict,
submerged, camouflaged,
who is to say
where is the trigger,

who is to say
which is my time

when sudden, unexpected,
as I speak so ordinarily,
the word simply
detonates,
explodes like my heart explodes

(going boom boom boom)

all my terms, my reference, my cover
blown

& I, even you, am, are
drenched like these walls

in all our bloody talk.

The Orphic tradition

Rossetti & the underworld

Bereft at the death
of his beloved Lizzie
         (o laudanum)
Dante Gabriel Rossetti
has his poems
interred there with her.

Later, on approach
from a publisher
         (o tempter)
he has them exhumed.

How, mister gravedigger
         (he innocently asks)
did she look?

Sunset Boulevard

In darkness
I am a dark creature.

Were I lit,
spotlit,

like any star
I would shine.

If I were lit
I would burn,

burn
as fame burns,

the bush,
the monk, burns.

Gloria Swanson,
as her burnt-out self,

is ashen,
yet her gesture

still flames -
hands, fingers

& nails -
those talons

sparking,
as she devours

her close-up,
one on one

in burnt-out
black & white,

is ashen,
is risen,

is Gloria.

II

In defence of my funding

Culture is a void,
taking all things,
turning them into itself.

As I look into the void
I look into a mirror,
the room still there behind me,

reflected over my shoulder
as proof. In time
to forget all proofs.

O culture, my culture,
aquarium of now,
I, *splendida inornata*,

gave no thought
to the masterpiece
muscling through my fins,

no thought
to the fish-fodder
raining down from above,

to those bubbling pearls
beaded like my bath-time farts,
bursting into light.

O culture, my darling

                    (waltzing my darling)

now too late

do I know my love,

now too late do I

recognise devotion, so deep so

compulsory. So thoroughly

drowned am I

that only now can

I fathom the reflection

of one so caught,

the casual world

making its pun against the glass.

Dream pedlary

for Grant Hackett
(via Beddoes & Baudelaire)

If a man is the sum
of his experience,
he lives in the past,
& the past, he knows,
is dead.

If he lives in the now
he may starve tomorrow,
learning nothing.

And if he lives
for tomorrow? Well,
it's the stone underfoot
that trips us.

For what then
to live?

We are often told
to live our dreams
but it's ambition they mean.

No one
really wants
to live their dreams.

No one
wants to live
the terror that is dream.

And if the terror is real
why not the dream,

not the ambition?

If a man would only
stand up in his *Speedos*,
& dripping
at that microphone

tell us straight
about his dreams, now
that would be heroic,
that would be Olympian.

The man dreams
he is a butterfly,
the butterfly
dreams he is a man.

Each of us indeed
might live his dreams

were it not
for these damned wings.

On my fifty-seventh birthday

To outlive Beethoven
seems impertinent.

Mozart, Chopin,
the Keatsian bloom?

To outlast a prodigy
is one thing. But Ludwig van,
the man himself, carries
the weight of edifice,
of rearing cliffs,
the carved rock-face staring back.

He has endured longer than the tedious stone,
cut off at the shoulders,
draped in eisteddfod ribbons,
plonked down on the sideboard.
He has listened in his stone deafness,
sage ancestor as the generations squabble,
unmoved.

On his brother's death
Beethoven pursued his sister-in-law
for custody of the boy. He pursued
her ruthlessly, relentlessly, to the grave
(his own). Beethoven died a monument,
miserable, petty, cold as the cold stone
that marks him.

Any of thirty-two piano sonatas,
any of nine symphonies, any string quartet
might have earned him this.

Even in this cheap plaster ornament
I can feel the stone standing tall.
I can feel the greatness of stone,
the cold thought of a monument
like something smashed up against.
I can feel the terrible will.

What does it matter to Beethoven
if *The Moonlight* chokes me up?

What is this matter
on which,
ruthlessly, relentlessly,

he pursues me?

Meet The Beatles

John met Paul met
George met
Ringo whose
mother had space
to rehearse.

History shits me like that -

what if the old woman
had lived in a shoe?

Ringo, a profile
made for caricature.

In my childhood
the 60's cartoons
taught me the songs
& the funny voices
but it was not
just records I wanted,
there was all sorts of stuff,

at Coles you could buy
a moulded plastic wig
that encased the head
like a helmet.

So when it all went weird
they lost me with
those beards, George,
John, the four of them
& the swami; even
this ten year old saw it -
can't buy me love.

Ten, twelve years later
I sat on Jeffrey St wharf,
John barely cold, the
Beatles still uncool.

Joy Division
was real death, poor
John mere misfortune,
the fans' give
& take.

But yes,
all we need is,
or was, love,

until Paul chimed in -
la la-la-la-la -
& the tune just killed it.

Or so goes
the serious reportage.

The punk at Central Station had

GOOD RIDDANCE
JOHN LENNON

in texta across his shirt.

I think of Paul
& all his good living.

I think of that bastard
Reagan, of miraculous

survival.

To Stanislavski

the method

Being one's own kitbag,
we reach inside. Is
this what is meant by
inner resources?

Grandpa had a shed
with peg-board on the wall;
all his tools, every one
hung there on its hook.

When he removed a tool,
any tool, took it down
with his hands, he
revealed an image,
outline, a silhouette
of that very tool
drawn there in its place.

When he found
the image of the hammer
revealed, I was punished.

As for you, gloomy,
forbidding old Russian,
artisan of archetype,
it takes more than a good nose,
not just any old structuralist
can build character, beat
by beat, action on action,
making it real.

We know where this
is going: to be
pieced together,
devised & contrived,
a made thing.

Yet Brando's more
real than I'll ever be.

I envy him his body,
having his lines provided,

by Tennessee fuckin' Williams.

For Randall Jarrell

They cannot agree,
as if readers of the one poem.

Accident, conclusive, states one source.
Suicide, another, yet more conclusive.

The circumstances will never be clear
(as if circumstances ever are)

opines, no, equivocates, the next.
Variously, these exercises in fact.

Reduced(?) to text,
your death is what we make it.

> *The birds come,*
> *sulphur-crested cockatoos*
> *come & sit & watch from the fence,*
> *or perch on my open window*
> *peering in.*
> *They come for their crackers,*
> *a cracker each*
> *which they take from my hand,*
> *which they eat from one claw,*
> *standing on the other.*
> *They eat distractedly,*
> *carelessly, the pieces & crumbs*
> *falling to the ground, wasted.*
> *They eat as if they know*
> *that I will always bring another.*

And so they come.
They come just to ensure
that I do.

I wrote that because
I was up early, reading you,
unable to sleep,

your poems opening up in the dawn.
I wrote that from *90 NORTH,*
for my white cockatoo snowmen,

their blazing yellow combs
in curiosity or alarm.
I wrote that because

it's what we do, turn
real stuff into poetry, hoping
to turn it back again.

I wrote that because
one text so depends upon another,
the whole flock lifting together,

rowdy, almost chaotic,
beating white like my laundry,
beating like my sheets to the wind.

I wrote that because
only alone, only in captivity,
do they speak.

Imitatio Dei

ghosting Graceland

The one Elvis impersonator
was Elvis himself.

From there is but mimicry,
idolatry.

Thus is devolved
from the *bright lights* of Vegas,
this suburban public bar,

where our next contestant,
in shamelessly sequinned shirt,

hitches his gut, hauls in a breath
& in all good faith
performs an atrocity upon

You Were Always On My Mind.

Three empty, one half full,
schooners puddle at my elbow,

a couple of dozen of us
littered amongst the tables.

Outside, a clutch of smokers
huddled against the rain,
peering in through the glass.

I ask myself again
what the hell I am doing here.

The authentic self is always,
by necessity, misplaced,
a joke at our expense.

We are, nonetheless, in on it.

If you say nothing
I will show you the same courtesy.

And so we find our limitations.

And so you cannot rely on friends
to tell you how flat you are.

Yet becoming like, seeking to become,
is the true nature of praise,
our meagre psalm to the grander scale,

with this public bar for Vegas,
our bedsit for Graceland,
where Elvis is real.

The Dear John letter

that's all she wrote

There is only the dust,
the grit, the particulars.

My camel
has got the hump,

recalcitrant beast that baulks
merely at the eye of a needle.

It would comfort me
to beat him, you, anyone,

but once I take out the carpets
I am assuaged.

In the cycling heat
I beat them instead.

They make the deep & hollow
guttural *humph*

of someone
doubled-up & winded,

of someone
gulping in dust. To poor

dear John:

herein all the violence
a poet is permitted,

his metaphoric head
& the wall it beats against

clad in ivy. I point again
my camel to the eye.

Again the rough beast baulks.

A sunburnt country

Sometimes,
even in a good film,
I don't want to watch,
I just don't want
to go through the process,
pleasurable though
that may promise to be.
I want to have watched,
to move straight to the end,
bringing the experience with me.
Then as the blind credits roll
I shuffle down the aisle,
through the chintzy foyer &
(how I love a matinee!)
out into the sudden Australian sun,
mid-summer, mid-afternoon,
the non air-conditioned
asphalt & traffic
coming at me like violence,
that I be overwhelmed
by sensation, submit
as if to conquest, unable
to secure my borders,
to protect my coasts,
the cancer nibbling into me
like a beach.

III

Mrs _____'s Hearing Aid

Mrs _____'s hearing aid is worth a month's pay.
It sits on the dresser when she goes to bed.
But Mrs _____ suffers dementia, delightfully so.
Mrs _____ lives with the fairies.
She will get busy in her room, any hour,
tidying, tidying, shoes in the fridge.
I check Mrs _____'s hearing aid at every opportunity.
I want to see it there on that dresser.
I need to know once & for all.
I did not ask for this responsibility.
The doors are locked behind me,
behind me & Mrs _____'s hearing aid.
I hear her scratching in her room,
nearly midnight, pecking away.
Of course she should be in bed.
Of course I should persuade her,
as I did not an hour ago.
I should check Mrs _____'s hearing aid.
I would prefer that Mrs _____'s hearing aid
were not worth a month's pay,
were not worth anything to me.
I prefer her deaf.
Deaf, she will tug at my shirt if she wants me,
will tell me with her eyes what it is,
with her knitter's fingers,
with the whole of her little-old-lady.
Deaf, she is animated.
Hearing, she just talks & talks.

An Awkward Moment

Mostly she's back where she grew up,
where she married, fed
four kids & a dozen shearers
three times a day.
Larlene was the matriarch
throughout her ninety-three years.
She has lost her wits, continence,
yet retains the will, she's tough.
In the end I just have
to put it to her blankly,
the smeared night-dress, slippers:
Larlene, you have soiled yourself.
She is shocked a moment. Then outraged.
I am foul-mouthed, vulgar, filth.
Did my parents not teach me?
That I would speak that way to a woman.
Any woman.
And in this house. To, to just stand there!
Me with towel, flannel, a fresh pad.

The Man Who Met Ezra Pound

I was cleaning his room
when out of nowhere he said
as if he'd just thought of it

> *y'know*
> *Aristotle maintains we are rational creatures*
> *but Freud would have the very opposite.*

I went on with my dusting.

I disposed of the urine bottle.

> *Yes* I said
> *Yes you could say that.*

*

The hum of the machine room
lends weight. A row
of government cars is parked
imperfectly along the brick
& concrete,
the drab public architecture
& motley rose-beds

where sprinklers piss against the walls,
where the tea-stain bore-water
hangs in the manured air,
in the morning sun,
tinted & bent,

hangs
like disinfectant in a corridor.

So too the wattle-bird
hangs upside down to pick
spiders from under the eaves,
a pair of honey-eaters
sees off a magpie, & lorikeets,
solar-powered, in the quick
colour of flight, burn that sun
for fuel.

They are raucous, welcome,
in the arms of the grandfather fig.

*

To shake the hand
of one who shook the hand.

*

Bent, hunched, so the eyes
are down, feet barely lifted
to walk. For one so in decline,
indefatigable, his lap
after lap of the corridors,
leant like a man into the wind,
spurning television, magazines,
every distraction but
Rachmaninoff's 2nd
& the Gideon

    here...kept here...with the rights of a child... a child has
    no rights...when he...whose name you know...sends money

    these doctors...the thing about doctors...an education...
    is not in itself...an education...if you get my...drift

Given time at the piano he provides
Alexander's Ragtime Band,
Ain't Misbehavin' & something
from Bach I can't name
all chopped to bits,
piecemeal,
in some unhinged
jazz.

        *

*they think I'm (taps the head)...don't know what I'm
talking about...THEY don't know...I on the other
hand...where do you go for conversation...for God's
sake...got a minute?...here's a limerick*

*

The past is filled with ruins.

The past would be wide open spaces,
would be arable land,

were it not filled with ruins

the past would be pasture.

It is not the broken landscape,
where once were walls,

it is not
the creatures that hide there,

the reptile
basking in thought.

It is not the sheer acreage,
the taking up of space,

as if we could somehow
make whole, as if we could

contain it all.

It is merely this overspilling,
the simple need to tell,

our ruinous attempts
to put it all back together.

*

*...old man by then...well past it...don't know how much
he took in...a few of us there...wanting to meet the great man ...he
was well away with it...the old fool...still, polite enough*

& getting up,
with the cord of his pyjamas
clutched in one hand,
he turns & gestures

someone best see to that...there's faeces on the chair

Jurisprudence

He's got to be ninety.

The saline drip
feeds into an arm.

The cupped mask
delivers oxygen.

He will die
on the outside.

He will die
in hospital pyjamas.

His bony wrists
rattle in their cuffs.

An ankle is chained
to the bed's metal frame.

To my clever remark
the armed guard just shrugs -

he did
kill somebody.

The Labours

She'll fight me.
If I try to get her up,
if I get the job,
she'll fight.

She will not hold back.
She'll kick, she'll scratch,
she'll get me by the hair
& spit till it drips

from me like yolk.
Her language bears
no repeating,
every wall blue.

I, of course, will
accept with
equanimity &
manoeuvre her somehow

from one incontinence
pad to the next, from
soiled pyjamas to fresh,
from this musty nursing

home bed to dinner &
back. I will not,
however tested,
respond rashly,

I will persist
with the futility of reason,
from the goodness
of my goody-goody heart.

Eventually, like the
end of time itself,
will come the end
of shift, & I

will be home,
dabbing disinfectant
on the marks in
my arm, washing

thick & sickened
saliva from my hair,
calculating a budget
from my one flat rate.

Solitaire

We put him in a vest
that has fake zippers,
button-holes that
clutch at nothing, clips &
buckles. We give him
these things to fiddle with
so he can be left safely
to himself, his ever
diminishing self.

IV

The watchmakers

The world is patient,
minute.

A pristine bench,
particular tools,
the lamp on its rangy elbow
staring down,

the wide-open device
flat-backed there,
shucked like a woman,
works exposed,

so intimately
engineered.

Faith is rewarded in kind,
is patiently made,
a small breakthrough in the shed,
a last piece fits into place
& something stirs
into life.

And yet we fail, we gods.

For all our tinkering
it is the mechanism itself
that ticks in triumph.

It makes a statement for itself,
counting off time.

Wailing wall

They jerk back & forth, up & down
like figures on a clocktower,
mechanical, clunking.

Theirs is a tradition of grief,
to wail at the ruin
two unforgotten millennia.

Bearded, ringlets,
they are a style unto themselves.

Black coats, hats, they are ravens
wound-up & pecking,
repeating, repeating, the one god.

They make the one holy gesture,
one pure enactment,
to make of the thing the ritual,
to make the ritual the thing.

Perhaps this is superior to thinking.
For what is it to think of God?
To think of thought itself.
To bang one's head against the wall.

Zoologic #4

Stoa

In doubt I praise
the given mind,

in my natural state.
I am there distinguished

amongst the creatures
&, I fear, my kind.

Fear, in turn,
would feed on doubt,

bring down like game
this uncertain joy.

What law protects me
protects my species.

For all our
wide parkland

we are beholden
to the warden.

I sniff the air.
I prick my ears.

I keep my faith
in check.

In doubt I praise
the given mind,

on all my fours,
free-grazing

the flat
awkward meadow

that is this verandah,
the verandah

on which I drink.

Pastoral

I am nibbling a weed, miles away,
alone with my thoughts, such as they are.
I am not thinking of them, of home.
I never really thought of myself as having a home.
A place amongst the flock perhaps.
But a place is not necessarily a home, I don't think.
In any case I am completely unprepared.
He sneaks up behind me as if I might run,
clutches me violently to him, head thrown back,
wild-eyed, yodelling to the flat papered-over skies.
He drops to his knees, rocking me, roughing me,
reciting crazily. I squirm to exhaustion.
In time he calms, regains himself,
his fervour passes as the storm over the pastures.
It has been a most baffling & traumatic experience.
I was nibbling a weed when there I was - snatched!
He has me now tethered about the neck.
I dig in my hooves & tug. On principle.
Good shepherd - for your lost sheep to be *found*,
surely she must consent.

Feudal

The house is infinitely abundant.
We run the taut lines of its skirtings,
we scuttle in its cupboards,
we line the walls with the softness of our fur,
our warm & nesting hearts.
From he who lives here, who built this house,
who Lords it over every room & corridor,
we shrink as from a sudden light.
For he who provides these our crumbs,
if there is gratitude in our quick rodent pulse,
it is encoded in our being a self-evident joy -
we suckle our downy young,
we are made numerous, in this house.
O but his footfalls do rattle us.
We are uncertain of our transgression.
In his presence we are fearful, hidden.
We freeze as he moves from room to room.
We listen as he lays his traps.

Silent Night

Weight
equals burden.

I am
the beast thereof,

the field I work
in turn works me.

As I
haul the long rows

I am
a drudge to glory,

my day
shin-deep in muck.

At night
in my stall,

deep
in sleep's pastures,

I dream,
at least imagine

I dream,
of that same field

under snow,
under falling snow,

blank & white
as that

first night
was blank & white.

I have never
seen snow.

Not real snow.
Not actually falling.

It all looks so clean,
so pure & white,

covering all.

It makes all things
pure, all things

white,
white as falling,

pure as gravity,
& gravity

itself
is weightless.

Old Testament

I made a god for myself,
some say *of*,
a grander version of self.
His temper roared, his law ruled,
his music brought the brickwork to tears
...*his kindness humbled his magnitude.*
I was doing the right thing
yet there came the realisation
that more was required. Down
in our vaults the gifts I brought him
shone even in darkness; ascending
into daylight became a diminution.
More & more I stayed there,
the private candle, the secret cubby,
all that I had crammed into there
radiant, glowing. It seemed right
against the wrong in the house.
Headlights swing into the driveway
& I am caught. In the suburban
night, dogs. I made
a god for myself.
I used my mind.
I used the materials provided.

Hermeneutic

He sends Word,
as if word were the thing,

the scapegoat word
that stands for the thing.

Yet we well know,
by all things stood for,

the word is not the word,
the word is another thing.

A mate of mine
meditated in a room,

seeking to negate the self,
seeking to negate

that mate of mine.
Me, I just leapt off a bridge.

Om.
Of all things to send

this unspeakable world,
He sends Word.

Theory

French they say
is the language
of love.
As a non-speaker
I resent the implication;
the French, they say,
have better words for it.
In the fug of translated prose
this English sticks.
I read the page over.
I read the page over again.
I read the page over & again,
its phrasing & rephrasing
giving benefit to the doubt,
as if Derrida weren't simply
full of shit, as if
we do inhabit a difference, even
if the French have better
words for it, untranslated,
working unspoken,
unforgiven on
the inner ear, working
like a cool idea, as if
a cool idea
makes a difference.
Yet it will not out,
this undifferentiated,
this indifferent love,
that the old man
has indeed

this much blood in him.
There is no word of difference
for this monolinguist.
There is none other,
even false.
There is one word,
one love.

At the heart of the world

The river is a god.
The river is a sewer.

There are pilgrims on television,
waist-deep in the polluted Ganges.

They immerse themselves in filth
yet come out clean, blessed.

Analgesia

Killing pain,
we shoot the messenger.

Pain is but the carrier,
the pigeon.

Yet pain says something.

Pain says there is something
you really should know.

Pain uses language
difficult to ignore.

Pain is our mother-tongue.

Pain is a collective noun.

So, yes,
we wanted God to suffer too.

Easter

Temples are built
stone on stone,
the cathedral's
steepling rooves
closing over.

He was not
lowered to the warm
mothering grave
but walled in
to the hollowed rock,
the hill's quarried side,
behind rolled stone,
in this holy pocket,
cellared wine.

When he woke he was,
in the perfect sense, alone.

In the cold, the dark,
the only source of light
was himself.

Pneuma

In your image
timekeeper, toymaker,
I am a facsimile,
doll. Moulded
as I am, I am
of another substance,
a portrait in a frame,
on a fridge, or
just the nagging idea that
something's lost, forgotten
to buy, something like
cigarettes, of
another time.
Who is it comforts
an old smoker?
Timekeeper, toymaker,
you give no guarantee.
Is there none to inspire
my plastic Barbie lips?
Is there only the curve
of my plastic Barbie breasts,
my plastic Barbie hips,
my hour-glass Barbie's
impossible shape
like the impossible shape
of a god?
Like something I just
can't breathe inside.

The paranoid lyric

When God made evil
it was to break
that endless monologue.

He drew a line. Having
drawn that line, He crossed,
turned to look on Himself.

He was not so pleased
as completed, that there
be Him & Not Him,
to be & not to be.

When God made evil
He lied.

Interventions

Tiddlers

A diver intervenes,
stripped to shorts,
drops like a predator.

Run little fishes!

I on my fish-legs am all
aflounder - so
hoist me in ridicule - (Lord!) -

I will be an old boot,
a weedy clump, a tatty shirt
atop your mast, I will say

you just got me as by-catch,

proud & singular
amid your drowning haul,
one amongst the little fish,

together, who moved as one.
I will be your anyone,
your manyone,

when you call, Lord,
call close & personal,
call for the one

in the beak of the kingfisher,
Your fisher of kings,
stripped to shorts.

Let that diver intervene
in the dawning surface,
to pick me out.

Seroquel

This cannot be a deafness,

as on this morning's train
the woman with headphones
flatly hums.

This cannot be an existing condition,

the true music kept from me,
the true word mumbled out of time.

I cannot be learned from diagnosis.

Say then that I am *sick of love.*
Say that love is its own relief.

Heal me with the true cure,
Creation scrawled in your illegible script.

Prescribe for me then your antipsychotic,
belief.

Blindside

I needed to see
but the light instructed my eyes,

then my eyes my brain &
- I was removed like a cousin.

It seemed that sight
might be a learned thing,

I needed to know that I saw.

I cannot then say
what I saw in him.

There was no way to know.

Unwashed,
heavy with street-grime,

his breath would stop a train.
That is the information I have.

By my own disgusted senses,

how he smelled & felt,
the weight of him,

the body's rumour handed down
like luggage to the platform.

Handed down, glory is glory.

I needed to see but he
came at me out of the light.

Stunned I just stood,
blind with metaphor.

The Gardener

Tangled little drunkard,
left traced across my doorstep,
last night's wayward way home.

I am glad not to have found you,
snail,

our meeting may have proved
quite crushing.

And you simply glad of me,
finding in my rambling, lazy patch,
a plenty.

With every garden, the gardener.

Hidden snail,
rolled down like a garage,
in your cell, tiny monad,

my boot is far from you.

I have merely a question
            (you & I at our chat),
one I cannot quite put.

It is something like
            how did you find me?
Something like.

My own cell is open with the dawn,
your fabled entirety
scribbled across the back step,

locating me here,
tippy-toed on the brink.

Do I stand?

Do I step out into the sky?

Waking At Night

It is as if I know the way.

When at night,
the same walls, doors, as today,
when lit.

I know my house.

I find my way in the dark.

I know to step forward, to turn,
as if I see, in this house,
in this night.

It is as if I know the way.

Through You, my darkness, my error,
I move.

Through You, my light.

The good review
for Carter

Scribes removed the vowels
from the name of God
as if to make that name
unspeakable, as if
to make that god
invulnerable. Go then
in fear of speaking. Go
& never speak the name.
Let it remain
on the tip of your tongue,
let it remain
like something removed.
You will speak
complete names,
for what complete
names are worth,
for protocol, etiquette,
style,
me, you,
table, chair,
that a manner of speaking
become a manner of being
that person,
product of speaking,
an ancestor named *Farmer*,
bucolic simpleton
whose own name
merely names his function,
a realist art
never less sacred or

separable: *et tu?*
(It is no paranoia,
no delusion,
any reader may destroy you)

YHWH